Lessons on Demand Presents

MW00897132

Teacher Guide and Novel Unit

for

The Girl Who Drank the Moon

By:

John Pennington

Cover Image:

Creative Commons Pixabay

The lessons on demand series is designed to provide ready to use resources for novel study. In this book you will find key vocabulary, student organizer pages, and assessments. This guide is divided into two sections. Section one is the teacher section which consists of vocabulary and activities. Section two holds all of the student pages, including assessments and graphic organizers.

Now available! Student Workbooks!

Find them on Amazon.com

Other titles include...

The War That Saved My Life

Esperanza Rising

Walk Two Moons

The Giver

One Crazy Summer

The One and Only Ivan

Flora & Ulysses

Island of the Blue Dolphin

The Little Prince

The Lightning Thief

Where the Red Fern Grows

And more........

Section One

Teacher Pages

Vocabulary

Suggested Activities

Chapters 1-3 Vocabulary

Kohl

Inexplicable

Façade

Contemplation

Hobbled

Luminous

Swale

Subdued

Millennia

Aghast

Pontifications

Clabbering

Chapters 1-3 Activities

Reading Check Question / Quiz:

Who lives in the woods that the people in the Protectorate are afraid of? The witch

What do the people of the protectorate do on the Day of Sacrifice? Leave a child in the bog for the witch.

Following the Day of Sacrifice for the Protectorate the Free Cities get what holiday? Star Child Day

What name does Xan give the child she decides to keep? Luna

Blooms Higher Order Question:

Distinguish how life is different for the Protectorate and The Free Cities.

Suggested Activity Sheets (see Section Two):

Character Sketch—Gherland

Character Sketch—Xan

Research Connection—Volcano

Pyramid—Rank the characters by age

Discussion Questions

Do you think any of the characters mentioned are villains? Why?

Why did Xan not take the baby to the free cities?

Why do the Elder continue the story of the witch in the bog?

Chapters 4-13 Vocabulary

Hypocrisy

Admonished

Inconsequential

Convalesced

Inert

Akimbo

Stasis

Obscure

Lament

Decoupage

Rapport

Proliferation

Chapters 4-13 Activities

Reading Check Question / Quiz:

Why is Xan worried about Luna growing up? Unable to control all of her magic.

Why is Antain going to be in trouble with the elders? He keeps making excuses to not attend the day of sacrifice.

Once Luna starts using magic what begins to happen to Xan? She begins to wither and die.

Who does Antain visit in the tower? Sister Ignatia and Luna's mother.

Blooms Higher Order Question:

You have one day of magical powers like Luna. What do you do with your day? Name a minimum of 10 things you would change and why you would change them.

Suggested Activity Sheets (see Section Two):

Character Sketch—Antain

Character Sketch—Grelk

Character Sketch—Fryian

Advertisement—Protectorate

Precognition Sheet

Sequencing—events from chapters 1-13

Discussion Question

Was Xan right in putting Luna to sleep?

Why was Antain having a hard time in the Protectorate even though he is a very agreeable person?

Chapters 14 - 24 Vocabulary

Prodigious

Trance

Retrospect

Fiasco

Chastised

Gravitas

Peevish

Apothecary

Tenacious

Belligerent

Unorthodox

Benevolent

Chapters 14-24 Activities

Reading Check Question / Quiz:

What was Luna no longer able to hear? Anything involving magic.

What profession does Antain pursue once he leaves the elders? Carpentry

What magical item does Fyrian retrieve? The Seven League Boots

What does Antain plan to do to save his baby? Kill the witch

Blooms Higher Order Question:

Draw what you think a map of the area should look like. Include all the locations mentioned in the story.

Suggested Activity Sheets (see Section Two):

Character Sketch—Luna

Character Sketch—Sister Ignatia

Chapter to Poem

Draw the Scene

Precognition Sheet

Who, What, When, Where and How

Discussion Questions

How does Antain transform during the story?

What do you think has been forgotten by different characters?

Chapters 25-32 Vocabulary

Dissuade

Gaunt

Anecdotal

Forensic

Duplicity

Deceit

Evasion

Observatory

Precise

Arabesques

Enumerated

Impervious

Chapters 25-32 Activities

Reading Check Question / Quiz:

What has changed about the madwomen? She has hope and can use magic.

What does Sister Ignatia plan to do to Antain? Kill him in the woods.

What item allows Luna to understand magic? The paper birds

What is Sister Ignatia also called? Sorrow Eater

Blooms Higher Order Question:

Create a magic item (similar to the Seven League Boots) and develop a back story for your item.

Suggested Activity Sheets (see Section Two):

Character Sketch— Ethyne

Lost Scene

Making Connections—Hope

Sequencing

What Would You Do?

Discussion Questions

Was Xan right in locking Luna's magic away?

Could someone like Sister Ignatia exist in the real world?

Chapters 33-47 Vocabulary

Wanderlust

Indolent

Imbued

Copious

Spectrum

Ambulate

Prevision

Chrysalis

Rheumy

Desiccate

Repellant

Implicitly

Chapters 33-47 Activities

Reading Check Question / Quiz:

What does Sister Ignatia feed on when she is loosing strength in the woods? The sorrow of the mother starling.

What allows Luna to get away from Sister Ignatia? The Paper Birds.

What allows Adara to get away from Sister Ignatia? The Seven League Boots.

What happens to Glerk and Xan at the end of the story? They return to the bog.

Blooms Higher Order Question:

Write down all the chapters and why the name is appropriate.

Suggested Activity Sheets (see Section Two):

Character Sketch—Adara

Create the Test

Top Ten List—Events

Discussion Questions

Compare how emotions are used in the story.

What do you think this world will be like in 500 years?

What will Luna do now that she can use magic?

Who are the heroes of the story and what makes them a hero?

Section Two

Student Work Pages

Work Pages

Graphic Organizers

Assessments

Activity Descriptions

Advertisement—Select an item from the text and have the students use text clues to draw an advertisement about that item.

Chapter to Poem—Students select 20 words from the text to write a five line poem with 3 words on each line.

Character Sketch—Students complete the information about a character using text clues.

Comic Strip— Students will create a visual representation of the chapter in a series of drawings.

Compare and Contrast—Select two items to make relationship connections with text support.

Create the Test—have the students use the text to create appropriate test questions.

Draw the Scene—students use text clues to draw a visual representation of the chapter.

Interview— Students design questions you would ask a character in the book and then write that characters response.

Lost Scene—Students use text clues to decide what would happen after a certain place in the story.

Making Connections—students use the text to find two items that are connected and label what kind of relationship connects them.

Precognition Sheet—students envision a character, think about what will happen next, and then determine what the result of that would be.

Activity Descriptions

Pyramid—Students use the text to arrange a series of items in an hierarchy format.

Research Connection—Students use an outside source to learn more about a topic in the text.

Sequencing—students will arrange events in the text in order given a specific context.

Support This! - Students use text to support a specific idea or concept.

Travel Brochure—Students use information in the text to create an informational text about the location

Top Ten List—Students create a list of items ranked from 1 to 10 with a specific theme.

Vocabulary Box—Students explore certain vocabulary words used in the text.

What Would You Do? - Students compare how characters in the text would react and compare that with how they personally would react.

Who, What, When, Where, and How—Students create a series of questions that begin with the following words that are connected to the text.

Write a Letter—Students write a letter to a character in the text.

Activity Descriptions (for scripts and poems)

Add a Character—Students will add a character that does not appear in the scene and create dialog and responses from other characters.

Costume Design—Students will design costumes that are appropriate to the characters in the scene and explain why they chose the design.

Props Needed— Students will make a list of props they believe are needed and justify their choices with text.

Soundtrack! - Students will create a sound track they believe fits the play and justify each song choice.

Stage Directions— Students will decide how the characters should move on, around, or off stage.

Poetry Analysis—Students will determine the plot, theme, setting, subject, tone and important words and phrases.

NAME:

TEACHER:

Date:

Advertisement: Draw an advertisement for _____

Chapter to Poem

Assignment: Select 20 words found in the chapter to create a poem where each line is 3 words long.

Title:

_____ _____ _____

_____ _____ _____

_____ _____ _____

_____ _____ _____

_____ _____ _____

NAME:

TEACHER:

Date:

Character Sketch

Name

Draw a picture

Personality/ Distinguishing marks

Connections to other characters

Important Actions

NAME:

TEACHER:

Date:

Comic Strip

Compare and Contrast

Venn Diagram

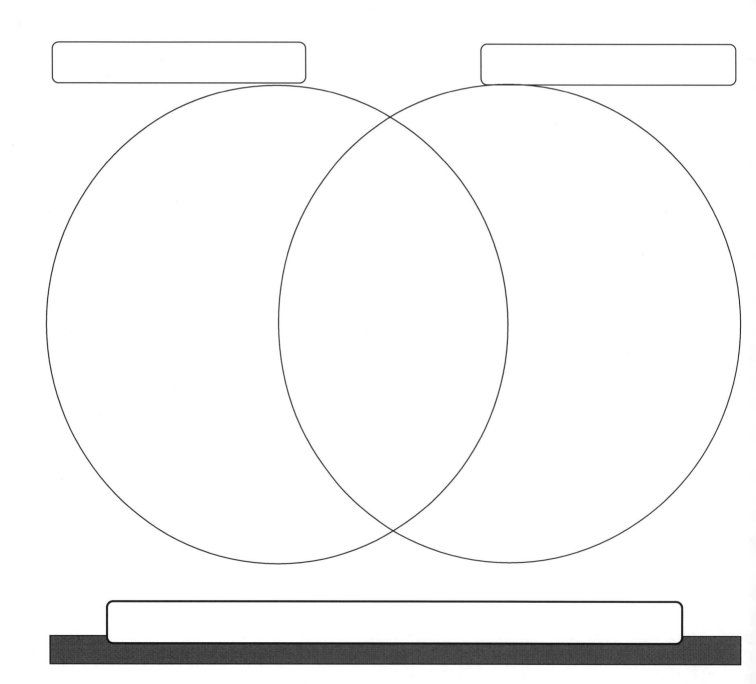

NAME:

TEACHER:

Date:

Create the Test

Question:

Answer:

Question:

Answer:

Question:

Answer:

Question:

Answer:

NAME:

TEACHER:

Date:

Draw the Scene: What five things have you included in the scene?

1   2   3

4   5

NAME:

TEACHER:

Date:

Interview: Who _____

Question:

Answer:

Question:

Answer:

Question:

Answer:

Question:

Answer:

NAME:

TEACHER:

Date:

Lost Scene: Write a scene that takes place between _____ and
_____

Making Connections

What is the connection?

NAME:

TEACHER:

Date:

Precognition Sheet

Who ?

What's going to happen?

What will be the result?

Who ?

What's going to happen?

What will be the result?

Who ?

What's going to happen?

What will be the result?

Who ?

What's going to happen?

What will be the result?

How many did you get correct?

NAME:

TEACHER:

Date:

Assignment: Pyramid

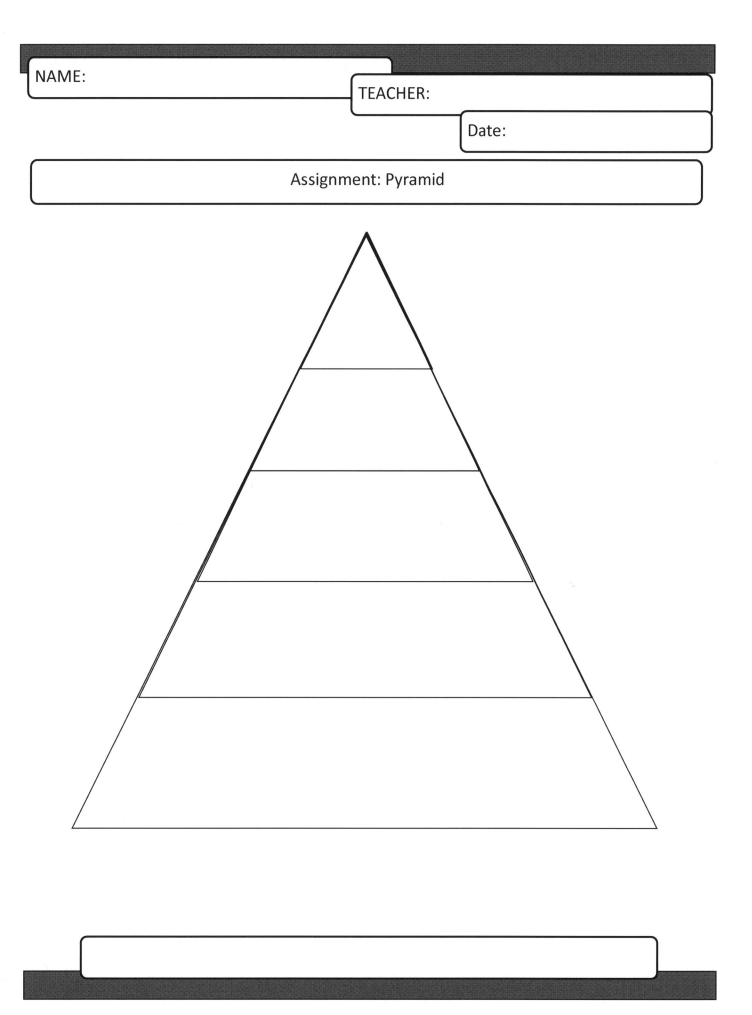

NAME:

TEACHER:

Date:

Research connections

Source (URL, Book, Magazine, Interview)

What am I researching?

Facts I found that could be useful or notes

1.

2.

3.

4.

5.

6.

NAME:

TEACHER:

Date:

Sequencing
or timeline

1.

2.

3.

4.

5.

NAME:

TEACHER:

Date:

Support This!

Supporting text

What page?

Supporting text

What page?

Central idea or statement

Supporting text

What page?

Supporting text

What page?

NAME:

TEACHER:

Date:

Travel Brochure

Why should you visit?

What are you going to see?

Map

Special Events

NAME:

TEACHER:

Date:

Top Ten List

1.

2.

3.

4.

5.

6.

7.

8.

9.

10.

Vocabulary Box

Definition:

Draw:

Word:

Related words:

Use in a sentence:

Definition:

Draw:

Word:

Related words:

Use in a sentence:

NAME:

TEACHER:

Date:

What would you do?

Character: _____

What did they do?

Example from text:

What would you do?

Why would that be better?

Character: _____

What did they do?

Example from text:

What would you do?

Why would that be better?

Character: _____

What did they do?

Example from text:

What would you do?

Why would that be better?

NAME:

TEACHER:

Date:

Who, What, When, Where, and How

Who

What

Where

When

How

NAME:

TEACHER:

Date:

Write a letter

To:

From:

NAME:

TEACHER:

Date:

Assignment:

Add a Character

Who is the new character?

What reason does the new character have for being there?

Write a dialog between the new character and characters currently in the scene.

You dialog must be 6 lines or more, and can occur in the beginning, middle or end of the scene.

NAME:

TEACHER:

Date:

Costume Design

Draw a costume for one the characters in the scene.

Why do you believe this character should have a costume like this?

NAME:

TEACHER:

Date:

Props Needed

Prop:

What text from the scene supports this?

Prop:

What text from the scene supports this?

Prop:

What text from the scene supports this?

NAME:

TEACHER:

Date:

Soundtrack!

Song:

Why should this song be used?

Song:

Why should this song be used?

Song:

Why should this song be used?

Stage Directions

List who is moving, how they are moving and use text from the dialog to determine when they move.

Who:

How:

When:

Who:

How:

When:

Who:

How:

When:

NAME:

TEACHER:

Poetry Analysis

Date:

Name of Poem:

Subject:

Text Support:

Plot:

Text Support:

Theme:

Text Support:

Setting:

Text Support:

Tone:

Text Support:

Important Words and Phrases:

Why are these words and phrases important:

Made in United States
Orlando, FL
04 February 2022

14448617R00026